UNDEFEATED

UNDEFEATED

A War Widow's Story of Faith and Survival

Wendy Taylor

RozzoCasa Press, Lower Burrell, PA 15068

RozzoCasa Press is an Imprint of AIW Press, LLC.
https://aiwpress.com

For the sake of privacy, all names have been changed in my story, with the exception of my own and my children's. This book is not meant to give professional advice in regards to my situation. If professional advice is needed, please seek the services of a professional.

ISBN-13: 978-1-944938-13-0

Cover photos by Meredith Melody Photography
Cover design by IDIM Designs
Military photos by courtesy of Arkansas National Guard

Personal military photos courtesy of
Chad Ambeau and Clint Sweeden

*To Michael, my soul mate, my best friend,
and my first love, whom I know I will see
again when God calls me home.*

*To Father Joseph, who walked through our front
door the day that we got the news and never
left our side. He held the torch of hope and light
for us when the three of us could not see our
way through the darkness of grief. Father
remains an important part of our family and will
always be cherished as he continues to walk
with us through our journey.*

You may encounter many defeats, but you must not be defeated. In fact, it may be necessary to encounter the defeats, so you can know who you are, what you can rise from, how you can still come out of it.

—Maya Angelou

It is not the critic who counts; not the man who points out how the strong man stumbles, or where the doer of deeds could have done them better. The credit belongs to the man who is actually in the arena, whose face is marred by dust and sweat and blood; who strives valiantly; who errs, who comes short again and again, because there is no effort without error and shortcoming; but who does actually strive to do   the deeds; who knows great enthusiasms, the great devotions; who spends himself in a worthy cause; who at the best knows in the end the triumph of high achievement, and who at the worst, if he fails, at least fails while daring greatly, so that   his place shall never be with those cold and timid souls who neither know victory nor defeat.

—Theodore Roosevelt
"The Man in the Arena," excerpt from the speech
Citizenship in a Republic (delivered at the
Sorbonne in Paris,
France on April 23, 1910)

CONTENTS

PREFACE

THE NIGHT OF POWER

Michael told me he was flying in Baghdad the last night of Ramadan; they called it *The Night of Power*. He said he saw shapes all around him through his night vision goggles that looked like baseballs on fire. He told me he watched the glowing spheres fly across the sky and thought it wasn't going to be good. The rest of the crew reported the same.

Then they "peeked" under their goggles and saw the flames were multicolored, not at all what they originally thought. They were not the threat they had feared; the people were just shooting Roman candles. As their flight progressed, they saw fireworks and more celebration for the end of Ramadan. He said no group was more joyous for the end of Ramadan than they were.

A LETTER FROM MICHAEL

365 days, 52 weeks, 24 paychecks, 12 months, 1 year

Mom and Dad:

Just a simple letter to let you know why I'm here, waiting to go to Iraq. I did volunteer for this. It was one of the hardest decisions I have ever made. Leaving the ones you love is difficult, trying to truly explain why is almost impossible. Wendy has supported me in all my decisions, even this one. She knows why I'm here and I want to be sure that you understand as well.

I love what I do. I know I can make a difference, not in the war nor the politics of why soldiers are there, but I can make a difference in the 42 soldiers that I'm responsible for and those troops that we will carry every day. That is why I'm here, simple as that.

It cuts me in half, my dedication to my profession and my love of my family. But in just 365 days, 52 weeks, 24 paychecks, 12 months, 1 year, I'll be whole again.

Love, Michael

1

A KNOCK AT THE DOOR

Some friends bring ruin on us, but a
true friend is more loyal than a
brother.

—Proverbs 18:24

It was a Sunday—uneventful for the most part. Earlier that day, I was at a birthday party with my eleven-year-old son, Justin, and my six-year-old daughter, Meredith. Home from the festivities, I began to make dinner. I had just started making spaghetti in the kitchen. The children were playing together upstairs. Just as the sauce began to simmer, there was a knock at the door. I thought nothing of it. I put down the spoon I had just used to stir the sauce, wiped my hands, and started down the hallway.

I pressed my eye to the peephole. A man in a military uniform stood there.

Why is he here?

———◆———

I opened the door and immediately felt my chest tighten—a chaplain stood behind the uniformed man. I couldn't quite grasp what was happening. Why they were on my front porch?

I invited the men in as the kids came running down the stairs, excited to see who our visitors were.

"Go back upstairs." I don't know why I told them that. There was something about the situation that made me feel that they shouldn't be in the same room with us.

I was right.

The casualty notification officer (CNO) and chaplain followed me down the hallway to the kitchen. We all sat down at the family table. And that's when the CNO, his eyes fixed on me, serious but compassionate, uttered the words a soldier's wife prays night and day she'll never have to hear.

"Mrs. Taylor, your husband has been in an accident." These are the first words I remember hearing.

He must be really hurt for them to come all the way here to tell me that.

"When is he coming home?" I asked. "Is he okay?"

He paused and said, "There were no survivors. All twelve perished."

I lost time and myself for a minute. My mind,

spirit, and soul just left. Unable to process the words that had just been placed on my heart, I blacked out completely. I came to with my hand on the officer's hand. I have no idea how it got there. Where did I go? I felt myself die inside in that instant.

"I need to leave a minute," I said. "I need to go upstairs." My voice was flat and dull. The CNO asked if I would like him to accompany me. I shook my head no. How many times have they had to watch this? How many loved ones have they seen disappear into shock and grief? I went to my bathroom and just stared in the mirror. I looked for answers as I studied my own face. I looked to make sure the person staring back was me—that this was not a dream. This wasn't how life was supposed to go. This wasn't what I had signed up for.

It isn't what anyone signs up for.

———◆———

I talked to you the night before. We Skyped each other. You were wearing the robe I sent you for Christmas. I could tell by your damp hair that you had just gotten out of the shower. Your hair was combed—parted neatly down the side; you looked so handsome.

We had a wonderful conversation that evening. Just before we said good-bye, you looked at me with so much love and warmth. You said so much to me with your eyes. It touched me. It also worried me. There was something about the way that you looked at me that made me feel uneasy, like I would never see you again.

———◆———

I have to tell my children. The thought hit me as hard as the initial blow. Staring at myself in the mirror, I realized I was not the only one who would have to deal with the news. I was not the only one whose life had just been turned upside down. I had just lost a husband, and my children had lost their father.

They didn't know that yet, and I did. And I would have to be the one to tell them.

What words do I use to tell them Daddy isn't coming home this time? How do I say that when we dropped him off at the airport, we said a forever goodbye? Justin was eleven, Meredith was six, and they no longer had a father. I was thirty-nine years old, and I couldn't fathom losing one of my parents. How were they supposed to handle such a traumatic load so soon in life?

I don't know how long I was in the bathroom. I do know I didn't scream or cry. I just stood there, staring at my reflection. Suddenly it hit me. I needed my mom and dad. That's all I wanted—my parents. I went downstairs where the two men still sat quietly, waiting to see what I'd do next.

"I need to call my parents," I told them as I picked up the kitchen phone.

"Do you need help dialing?" one asked.

"No." It seemed a strange question to ask. He just wanted to help me in some way, I imagine. He couldn't, though. I needed my parents.

My mom answered the phone.

"You need to come here right now," I said.

She didn't ask me any questions. She just said okay and hung up the phone.

The officers left not long after that. I assured them that my parents would be there soon—that I'd be fine. When the door closed behind them, I called my precious children downstairs. I had them sit on the couch. As I went down to my knees, I asked in my heart, *How much more, God? How much more do I have to do?*

"Is Daddy okay?" Meredith asked.

"Daddy has been hurt," I told them. "Was it bad?" Justin asked.

I paused. My heart shattered. I knew I was about to tell them something that would change them forever. All I could think was how much I didn't want to do it. I didn't want to do that to our innocent children. But I had to. I looked into their beautiful eyes and said the hardest words I have ever uttered.

"Yes, your father died." The words didn't seem to belong to me.

Someone told me once when you tell children their parent has died in war, you have to be sure they understand that parent is never coming home. You can't say, "Daddy was hurt" or "Daddy was in an accident." You have to be clear. I knew as hard as it was, it was the way I had to say it. I couldn't offer anything open-ended.

Death was final; my words had to be as well.

Keeping the family together while Michael was gone had been hard enough. And now I was kneeling in front of my children, telling them Daddy would never come home to us—not the way he used to.

That moment I told them was the most excruciating part of losing Michael. That moment awoke me from my numbness and shock and threw me into a tailspin of devastation. I will never forget the look of disbelief on their faces. That alone ripped my soul to shreds. It was in that moment I felt my old self leave. Michael took who I was with him when he died. I was left a shell of that person. I felt God place that cross on my back—my heavy cross to bear.

Justin had gone upstairs to his bedroom at some point to be by himself. Our priest, Father Joseph, dropped by soon after we had found out and proceeded to go upstairs to check on him.

Later that day, the priest pulled me aside and told me about his conversation with Justin.

"Where are we going to live?" Justin asked Father. "How are we going to pay the bills?"

If the situation wasn't heartbreaking enough, my son, who was not yet even in junior high, was concerned about how we would pay bills now without his father.

"You don't need to worry about that," Father Joseph assured him. "Everything is going to be fine."

His words splintered the already-shattered pieces of my heart.

As soon as the officers left, two of Michael's close friends, Sergeant Major Grace Henderson and Major Nick Dumas, who were stationed stateside, came to the door. They had been sitting in a car outside my house, waiting for the CNO and chaplain to leave. They didn't want me to be alone after I got the news. I was sitting on the couch when Nick came and squatted next to me.

"This can't be happening," I said. I wasn't really saying it to him as much as I was to myself. "He was supposed to be home next week. He's supposed to be home for Valentine's Day." I just kept repeating those words. "This can't be happening."

"It's just so strange," Nick replied. "I just talked to Michael a couple of days ago. It's just so odd. He was here one day, and now he's suddenly gone. I just talked to him."

Nick must have said that half a dozen times while he was there. "I *just* talked to him."

"I know." I felt just like Nick did, and then some.

"I want you to know I am going to Dover so I can fly back with Michael," Nick told me.

"Thank you." It was all I could say in that moment. This action meant so much to me, but it took all I had for me to muster up those two words.

"He was like a brother to me," he said.

The next thing I remember is my mom and dad coming through the front door. When they walked in, I was silent. I looked at my mom and shook my head from side to side. That was all; she knew. She gasped and covered her mouth with her hand. Her legs buckled a little under the pressure of the news. I don't remember anything else that happened in that moment.

I had to look at my children, knowing that our lives would never be the same. I had to answer their questions when I didn't necessarily know the answers. I had to comfort them when I felt like crumbling. That is what a soldier's widow is called to do. That does not make it easy.

Shortly after I told my children, I curled up on

the couch beneath a blanket. My parents must have informed the rest of the family. People were coming and going, but I had no idea who was there because my head was down the entire time. I would only know someone was near me because I would feel their weight beside me on the couch. I never looked up to see who it was. Sometimes the person sitting next to me would ask me a question.

"Have you eaten anything, Wendy?" "Have you had anything to drink today?"

I didn't know how to answer that. The simplest of questions made no sense to me.

"I just can't be here without Michael," I'd mutter every now and again, leaning up on one elbow, my eyes still focused on the ground. I've been told I started to call my mom *Mommy* and my dad *Daddy*, although I don't remember this. Everything went by in a blur. The most I remember is being on the couch the following morning while my mom sat on the floor next to me, saying, "I'm so sorry."

I couldn't say anything, however. I was numb.

I had never felt that kind of heartache in my life. I thought I might die in my sleep from a broken heart, it hurt that bad. As I lay there, I prayed God would take care of my children if I didn't wake up.

When it was finally time to go to bed, I went up to our bedroom. Instead of putting on pajamas, though, I opened the closet door. I stared at his uniforms hanging there, waiting for him to come home and wear them again.

Michael and I had been married for twenty years. I went from my parents' home to our home. He had been there to guide me, protect me, and love me. And I was suddenly left with a closet full of uniforms that would never be worn again. I put the arms of one of the uniforms around my shoulders as it dangled on the hanger. I wanted to feel like he was holding me. I stood there for some time, crying into the chest of the uniform as if it were Michael standing there, holding me, comforting me through the worst time of our lives.

I needed him so badly. My whole body hurt so much. I stomped my feet, and for the first time, I screamed.

"Where are you! My God, where are you? Why did you leave me? I'm so afraid. I need you! Our children need you! I can't live without you. Why did those people kill you? They just killed you, like you didn't matter. They didn't even know you, and they killed you. Why?"

I went upstairs that second day to take a bath and just to get away from all the people and noise in my house. I needed some alone time. Evil decided to try to get me at my lowest point. I got in the tub and lay down, putting part of my head underwater to cover my ears so I could have silence. Suddenly I found myself sitting up slowly, as if in a trance. I felt numb. My feelings were nonexistent, and I didn't remember that I had children, parents, friends, or anything. It was as if my brain had been wiped of everything, and I was just a shell of a person. I watched my right hand reach over to a razor blade that had been left on the rim of the tub. I slowly picked it up, still with no feelings—nothing. I was null and void. I started to carry the razor in the direction of my left wrist and placed it there. Suddenly a huge presence came into the room and "woke" me up. It was the presence of God.

I put the razor down, lay back into the water with my ears covered, and said quietly to Him, *I surrender. I give you my children, my home, my finances. I give you my life. I give you everything.*

I remember when our children were born. It was the most beautiful and euphoric feeling in the whole world. Seeing your child's face for the first time is truly a miracle. Handing Justin and Meredith over to their father when they were born was such a bonding time for both of us. Handing over something beautiful and sacred for my husband to hold is a moment in time that will forever be etched in my mind.

When Michael died, I realized that children, spouses, close family, and loved ones don't really belong to us. They are gifts from God that we have for only a short time. God trusts us with his children. This was such a profound realization for me in my depths of grief. Michael was a gift God entrusted to me. He loved me enough to share Michael with me and to allow me to have twenty wonderful years with him. He also gave us two beautiful children, precious lives we made together.

When I look at Justin and Meredith now, I see Michael. I know that part of him still walks the earth. He smiles through Justin and reaches me through our son's movements that are so much like his. He shows his playfulness and laughter through our daughter. What a beautiful vision to see. Those gestures and actions are what I have left of Michael.

My children are my life, my whole heart. They kept me moving and striving for a better morning when I could not go one day without crying. They are my inspiration and hope for the future.

My children saved my life.

In the depths of horrific grief, they gave me something to live for. They were my purposes in life. My children and God have helped me to become a better person. And for that, I am very grateful and humbled.

I had a vision of handing over Michael to God like I handed my children to my husband years earlier. I handed my newborns over to their father, I then had to hand over my husband to his Father. Our Father in heaven. I remember having this vision soon after Michael died and asking for our Blessed Mother to take good care of him for me. This thought gave me a little moment of peace through the haze and confusion of those times.

I thought I knew what surrendering meant before I lost Michael, but I didn't until that moment in the bathtub. I believe true surrendering happens when we have nothing left but God. That's when He can do His best work, because nothing is in His way. Your spirit and soul are completely open to being filled by the Holy Spirit and nothing else.

I was born again through God. A transformation to a higher level of understanding of our Father. Michael took the old Wendy with him, and God filled me back up with a better version, even if, at that time, I couldn't recognize it through my grief.

When traumatic loss in life happens suddenly and violently, it will change you. The few days immediately after this loss, you will become aware of a fork in the road through the fog of your grief. It may peek out through a suffocating haze of pain and confusion, but it is there.

You have a choice to make when you hit it—you can give up or get up. I chose to survive and to keep my children's heads above water. To carry them while God carried me. This happens one tiny step at a time, and I mean tiny.

The first thing I did when I realized I wanted to fight back was head for the garage, where Michael's truck was.

I stood in the doorway to the garage, barefoot and in pajamas, and I looked at his truck. I climbed in the truck and felt fear, like it was my first time to drive. I knew my mind wasn't working right—I was foggy from everything that had just been dropped into my life. But I also knew that I wanted to fight back. So I pushed the fear back, and I turned the key.

"This is for you, Michael!" I called out as I pulled out of the garage. "I'm fighting back!"

I didn't go far, just around the neighborhood a couple of times. But as I drove, I felt like Michael was there with me. The familiar hum of the engine reminded me of the countless times we would take the truck out for a drive with no destination in mind. We would roll the windows down and just take in the sights. We enjoyed the quiet time when it was just the two of us, and also the intimate conversations we could have in the cab of that truck.

I wanted to capture those moments somehow. I wanted to recreate them so I could feel him in some small way. And I did.

It was the smell of the truck—it still smelled like him—and the way it sounded and moved. Those things made me feel his presence again. And I thought about how his fingerprints were all over the truck, the steering wheel especially. My hands were right where his had been. My back rested where his always had when he was in the driver's seat. All I could think was how I just wanted one more drive with him—just one more. If I could just see him one last time; if I could touch him, wrap my arms around him, and tell him how much I love him. But I knew that taking his truck out for a drive would have to do, until I made my way to heaven to be with him again.

I also knew one more time wouldn't be enough. I knew that I'd want one more over and over again until we were too old to go on. I knew I wouldn't be able to let go if God granted me one last time. I shouldn't have to. We were young. We still had decades until we should have to say goodbye.

So I decided I wouldn't say goodbye. I would hang on to Michael in every way I could. And I knew that his spirit would always be with me forever, so I didn't need to let go. I still needed him, and I wasn't ready to do that. So while I would learn to live without him here physically, I would never let go. I would move through my grief but not give him up. Even as the days ahead meant accepting the reality of his death, again and again, I clung to Michael.

2

THE STAGES OF GRIEF

No one has greater love than this: to lay down one's life for one's friends.

—John 15:13

I didn't want to believe Michael was dead. I remember asking my casualty assistance officer (CAO) Major Ezra Jones to show me the paperwork used to notify us—I needed to see Michael's name, and wanted to look at the Social Security number. He brought it to me later that day, and I quickly looked at the yellow highlighted area with his name and number on it.

I was having trouble accepting his death. Did they make a mistake? Was it really him? Did someone take his place on the aircraft without them knowing? Did he really escape and was hiding somewhere and they just didn't know? He couldn't really be gone. He's my soul mate.

As the reality that Michael was, in fact, gone set in little by little, I started to see life in such a different way. It's like a light came on all of a sudden. The light made me see how so much that we focus on is trivial.

And I became intolerant of the trivial.

This all came to the surface the day my mom dragged me out of the house to get a black dress for Michael's funeral. I should have been buying a dress to celebrate his homecoming, but instead I was looking for something to mourn him in. This made the entire ordeal more than unbearable.

As I was out shopping, I got angry at how focused everyone was on the most insignificant things. I saw people buying new shoes and asking if a shirt would shrink after it was washed, and all I could think was, *Who cares?* I wanted to yell at everyone, *None of this matters!*

I felt like I was losing my mind. I also felt like I never wanted to go out into public again. I knew it wasn't these other people's faults, but I couldn't stand to be out among people who had no idea what I was feeling. All of these people's lives were just going along, but mine had stopped. I felt more alone than ever when I'd be in crowds.

I couldn't be out in public, and I also couldn't sleep for days and weeks after I found out. This sounds strange, but the movie *Under the Tuscan Sun* got me through that little period when it seemed nothing else would. I would watch it morning after morning when I couldn't sleep. I just sat on my feet right in front of the TV, all alone in the living room, and watched the movie. My mom had bought it for us to watch together, but I popped it in the first night because I was restless. As I lost myself in the plot, I felt the pain subside, if only a little. That movie became part of my routine.

Grace helped when *Under the Tuscan Sun* could do no more for me. She was there with me to keep me company and to help where she could. I had developed a strong bond with her because, in some ways, she could grasp my pain. She lost her son David in a car accident, and her heart hurt terribly for him. We shared that traumatic connection. We would talk and cry together on the phone. She felt the pain that I was feeling. We understood each other. We needed each other.

Sometimes I would just sit on the floor in my bedroom and talk with her until I couldn't talk anymore. We both knew how it felt to be misunderstood in our grief, how people wanted us to be our old selves. We didn't know how to tell them that it would never happen; our old selves had gone. It was a comfort to have someone there who got that—someone I could talk to about how much I had changed forever because of my loss. She truly was a godsend. She was an angel who talked to me through all the phases of my grief.

The day before the funeral, I called my friend Cassandra to come upstairs so I could tell her something. When she got to the top of the stairs, I told her, "I swear I keep hearing 'I'm alive, I'm alive!' in my heart."

"He is alive, just not the way you want him to be." She wrapped me in her arms.

But I didn't want to listen to her. I kept fighting the thought that he was gone, even though somewhere deep inside me, I knew it was true. I was looking for anything to prove otherwise and just couldn't find that something.

Cassandra was a sweet and loving friend from church. She sat with me the day I was notified, and I remember her putting Meredith on her lap while sitting in front of our Sacred Heart altar. I often think of how much sorrow she must have carried at that moment while she held my daughter and watched me pace back and forth in shock. She also handmade a beautiful life-size rosary that I had Ezra place in Michael's casket before he was buried. She was a true blessing from God.

At some point, the Army got all of Michael's things back to Arkansas so his friends could bring everything to me. All of his belongings were in big plastic containers. As Nick and Grace brought them in one at a time, it was hard to believe that was all I had left of him. Instead of getting my husband back from his tour, I would only get his things. I told Grace the one thing that I really wanted at the time was the robe that I had sent him for Christmas.

This was the last thing I saw him wearing when we Skyped for the last time the day before he was killed. They brought all the containers to me and placed them in the front room. I spent hours just sitting and grieving, looking at all his things. Nick asked me if I wanted him to move the boxes upstairs somewhere out of the way, but I told him no. I wanted to sit around them all day because it made me feel close to him. Plus, I could smell his scent come off the containers just a little bit.

"Do you know which container the robe is in?" I asked Grace as Nick toted the boxes into our house.

"I'm not sure."

We began to look together.

It didn't take long before I found it. I slowly pulled it out as they sat with me and watched. Before his belongings were sent to me, I had specifically requested they not wash the robe so his scent would still be on it.

"Did they do what I asked?" I clutched the robe. "Did they not wash this?"

"I'm pretty sure they did just what you asked," she said.

I put it up to my face and breathed in until my lungs couldn't hold any more air.

I was relieved to find that his scent was still on it. Then I began to cry. Grace and Nick sat with me as I buried my head in his robe and sobbed. I could sense their sorrow as they sat with me. I'm so glad I had people who cared not only for Michael but also cared about me and the kids. I will hold these precious moments in my mind forever, and I will always be thankful for the love and care that our Army family showed us in our time of need.

I had told Grace that the one thing I really wanted was Michael's robe, but that wasn't the case. Of all the things I got back that day, the thing I wanted most was Michael's wedding band. And it wasn't there.

I knelt down on my knees in my bedroom one night and asked God to somehow give me his wedding ring. I was very aware of how bad the accident was and had been told about the fire. I knew something as small as a wedding band would be almost impossible to recover from a helicopter crash.

I just needed something that was on him the day he died, and so I begged God for Michael's wedding band. I immediately heard a whisper in my aching heart that I would have it.

After that, I told people I would get the wedding band back somehow. Everyone around me said it was not possible. They reminded me the aircraft had burned up and nothing would be left.

But each time, I would reply, "God told me I would have it." This is one of those moments when I stood alone with God. I had a knowing, and I didn't care if anyone believed me or not. I know what our Father told me, and that's all I needed.

———◆——

For me, and for anyone who loses a loved one, grief comes in stages. It isn't something you just get over after a few months. The void left when you lose someone you thought you couldn't live without can never be truly filled. It may become less encompassing, but it is always there. And when you lose a spouse in a war, there is a separate set of reminders that come with the mourning process. For all people who lose loved ones, holidays are tough—Christmas, birthdays, New Years, Thanksgiving, anniversaries—all these are reminders that your life is forever changed. But for soldiers' widows, there is also Memorial Day, a national holiday created to remember fallen soldiers. I am so appreciative for this day, now more than ever. But appreciating it does not mean Memorial Day isn't particularly hard for me and my family.

The first Memorial Day after I lost Michael, I was extremely sad. I remember I felt so completely alone even though I was with my entire family. Seeing people smile was hard. Memorial Day is a day to honor our soldiers who have given the ultimate sacrifice for our nation, but that first Memorial Day without Michael I realized it seems few remember that. Of course, because I am a military wife, our family always recognized what Memorial Day really meant But when my husband became one of the fallen, I began to see how few people understood what that day really meant for our country and for the families of those who lost their lives defending our freedom. It also occurred to me that even for those who do keep the purpose of the last Monday in May in mind, they spend only one day a year remembering the lives lost in war.

For me, every day is Memorial Day. And it always will be.

It is 2016 now. I have spent nine Memorial Days as a soldier's widow. Does it get easier? No, not really. I spent the last Memorial Day as I have spent all the others—with my family surrounding me and supporting me. We went on a little family weekend getaway to my parents' lake house, just as we always do. It is supposed to help me focus on what I have. These little vacations are supposed to keep me occupied as I am reminded everywhere that a war took my husband—that a small group of radicals who have no respect for human life changed my family's life forever.

I sat with my family and tried to soak in the moment, but as we sat around chatting at the dining-room table, their words began to fade out into a hum—a hum of different tones of noise. My ears seemed to become deafer as I noticed nothing but that one empty chair. That chair will never be filled, and I will never take for granted what it means to die for a country because my husband did. Like I said, for me, every day is Memorial Day.

As I stand before the American flag, I realize how it encompasses all that surrounds me. Its wings of color roll and flap as the voices of ones gone before us whisper their former lives, the blood of their sacrifices now intertwined in the threads of red before them.

I stand in admiration and feel indebted to carry on the memory of my husband, Major Michael Taylor, and all the fallen before and after his final flight to heaven. His memory will forever flow through my soul as I continue to walk this earth and speak his name proudly and boldly. For a man of his character and nobility has left a mark on many of us left behind. Let us share the impression of that mark with others so his name will forever ring in the ears of many. His story is one of great sacrifice and love for his country.

If you stand in silence long enough before the flag of red, white, and blue, you shall hear his voice also as it whispers through the threads of red. God bless all of our fallen soldiers, and God bless America.

3

EXTENDED GOODBYES

For we know that if the earthly tent we live in is
destroyed, we have a building from God, an eternal
house in heaven, not built by human hands.
—2 Corinthians 5:1

Once I decided I'd survive, I had to ease my way
back into life. It started with me telling myself
every morning to put my feet on the ground, get
my children ready for school, and drive them
there. I told myself to get in the shower every day.
I let the hot water run over my head and back, and
then maybe I dried my hair if I was up to it.
Eventually I wore something other than pajamas.

If the grief hit me hard one day, I learned to
allow it to take its course, and I waited for it to
pass. What else could I do? I had to remind
myself to eat to keep my strength up so I could
take care of my children. I opened the blinds, just
a little, to let the sunshine in.

I took naps if I was tired, and I learned not to

feel guilty about it. I learned not to feel obligated to pick up the phone every time. You have to allow yourself the freedom to not have guilt. You are the one grieving. You don't owe anyone an explanation. You get to be silent when the time calls for it.

I also had help from loved ones. There was one friend in particular, Jessica, who was my rock when I needed her most. Her husband, Paul, was a good friend of Michael's. He was deployed with Michael and was there the day of the accident. She came to see me the day that I found out. She walked through the front door sobbing so hard. I could see she felt my grief. We hugged each other for dear life, not knowing what to do.

She came to see me every single day while I was bombarded with paperwork, visitors, and decisions to make, most extremely difficult. She was by my side, and I could tell she truly loved me and wanted to help.

The first time I decided to eat, she was there. It was potato soup a neighbor had brought over. We had both lost weight, and people kept telling us we needed to eat. Finally, one evening, we sat down next to each other and ate our soup in silence. We developed a bond that needed no words. It started when she walked in that front door the first day and we hugged. We needed each other, and we knew it.

My only goal was to make my children feel safe and secure at home. I talked to myself every day, encouraging my spirit to keep moving and not give up. Every time the grief knocked me down, I got back up. I allowed myself to grieve at my own pace and face it head-on. This is the only way to make it through a dark time. You can't run from it because it will find you—always. I had to let the grief take its course.

I also learned how to appreciate life more, even in my pain. And there were so many phases of pain I went through. New wounds would open that made the initial visit from uniformed soldiers come rushing back to me. One of the most difficult of those wounds was the day that my husband finally came home.

It was time to pick Michael up from the airport. It was time to welcome him home. I got ready for my husband, like I had so many times before. I wanted to look nice for him even though I knew I wouldn't get to physically touch him or see him. My CAO Ezra picked me up in a van to take me to meet Michael at the army post. We pulled in, and we waited as his plane landed. He was the only passenger except for Nick, who had volunteered to fly back with him. He considered Michael a brother and watched over him for me during my husband's final trip home.

Throughout his career, Michael always made sure his soldiers were taken care of, and he took his responsibility as a commander very seriously. He was a man of noble character and integrity. He was a good leader for his soldiers, just like he was for our family. Now his soldiers were paying him the respect in his death that he had showed them in life. They even made sure he was never alone.

I started to feel numb and light-headed as the plane landed. I felt like I was outside of my body and might pass out. The van door slowly opened, and Ezra helped me out. I felt like I was watching myself move toward the plane. I could hear my boots pounding down on the ground beneath me as I made my way across the flight line, but I couldn't feel my feet. I felt like I was floating—the sound my boots made seemed removed from me. Everything felt so detached. My knees suddenly gave out, and Ezra and Jessica grabbed my arms to keep me from falling.

I lifted my head and looked across the flight line. There, in front of me, was a row of Michael's friends in uniform. They all stood at attention as I walked toward the casket. I didn't call it a casket then; I called it his "bed." I couldn't bring myself to say that word. It seemed so final and unacceptable.

His friends held the casket; they lined both sides of the last bed Michael would have as I slowly approached them. It was so quiet all around me. All I could hear were the flags the Patriot Guards held flapping in the wind as Michael's friends stood in formation.

When I finally got to him, I placed my head on top of his "bed" and whispered, "I'm so sorry. I'm so sorry." All I could do was apologize to him. "Michael, I'm so sorry," I repeated. I could hear soft crying around me as I kept my head on his bed. I couldn't keep from saying, "I'm so sorry."

It wasn't the welcome home I had imagined. I wanted to be able to run up to my husband in the airport and jump into his arms as he let my feet dangle. Michael was over six feet tall, and I am not much over five feet, so when we hugged, he would lift me from the ground. I wanted to run my hands through his thick dark- brown hair that had been in a military cut for as long as I could remember. I wanted to feel his strong, graceful fingers clutch me. I used to watch him turn pages in a book just to watch his fingers. I would not get to see those fingers ever again, or look into his hazel eyes, which always looked very green when he wore certain shirts. I wanted to wrap my arms around his neck and tell him I loved him as I nestled my face in his neck and breathed in his scent—a scent

I would only get from the belongings shipped back in plastic containers from Iraq. I wanted to watch him bend down and hug our children and see the three of them smile at each other. I wanted that feeling of knowing I was safe because he was home and would make everything okay.

I didn't get that. I didn't get my turn.

———◆◆———

I was in the pouring rain with Michael. We were outside, and the moon was full so I could see his face well. He stood there looking at the sky. The rain danced down his face as he began to sob. He said he felt so lost in his life. He was nineteen at the time, and he just didn't know which direction to go. He fell down to his knees on the wet ground. I knelt down beside him and grabbed him, wrapping him tightly in my arms. I kept telling him that we would figure this out together, that I wasn't going anywhere. I insisted that he just follow his heart.

The decision was made that night in the rain with our knees in the mud. He was going to enlist in the military. I knew right then that his life was getting ready to change forever. I supported him one hundred percent. My gut told me that was his calling. We stood up together. He told me he loved me, and we began a journey together.

Soon after that, I drove him to the bus station,

and he went to basic training. I told him I would wait for him, and I did. Six weeks later, he asked me to come to Biloxi, Mississippi, and marry him. I said yes. We got married on July 22, 1986, in a little courthouse there in Mississippi. I called my family from a phone booth nestled there on the beach to give them the news. He then took me to the tiny apartment that he had gotten for us, and I had never been happier. We were dirt poor, but we didn't care. We had each other, and that was all that mattered.

We chopped down our own Christmas tree that year because we couldn't afford to buy one. We bought a few ornaments to put on it but no lights. The tree stood in a small wicker container I already had. I still have a couple of those ornaments and put them on my tree every year. When I look at them, I'm reminded of simpler times and how happy we were with nothing. We were both nineteen years old, but even at that tender age we knew we were soul mates. As long as I could lay down my head on his chest every single night, I was at peace.

———◆———

I thought if I continued to be supportive of you and be here for you as you took on all the responsibilities of being a commander, one day when this hectic period was over, I would eventually get my turn.

I stepped aside willingly so you could do your duties and take care of your soldiers to prepare them for war. I knew the importance of this and wanted to be a loving and supportive wife for you. I wanted you to fulfill your passion of being a Black Hawk pilot and be happy with your accomplishments.

Your happiness was very important to me. Your happiness was my happiness.

I would always be there for you and our children, no matter what. You were my soul mate, and I loved you and still love you with all that I am. I thought we'd get to live out that love for so many more years than we got. I thought a day would come when I wouldn't have to say goodbye again and await your return.

But that isn't what happened.

I said goodbye, for an indefinite amount of time, and now I just wait for our reunion. If I get it right here on earth, then I will get my turn in heaven with you.

———

A couple of days before Michael's funeral, Father Joseph thought it would be a good idea to sit in the church by myself for a little while. I had not been in the church since I was notified of Michael's death. He thought it might help me to sit in the pews and pray, or just be present, to get used to being in the church again before the funeral. He was afraid if my first steps back in the church were for the funeral, I may never come back inside because I would feel like I was walking back into the funeral once I returned for regular mass.

I agreed with him. I didn't want the one place that offered me so much peace to be a place I couldn't stand to walk into. So I decided before I walked in to church dressed in black with all eyes on me, a soldier's widow, I would take a day and walk in just as Wendy, a mourning Catholic reaching out to God and our Blessed Mother.

Ezra came to pick me up from home and took me to the church to meet our priest. We pulled up on the driveway that went right to the front doors of the church. It struck me that the driveway was used for vehicles during funerals—hearses. I couldn't get that thought out of my head as we parked at the front doors. Father opened the church for me, and I walked toward the front and sat in the second row. He gave me his phone.

"Call me when you are ready to leave," he said. His voice was soft and comforting. His eyes were sad but full of compassion. He left me alone and made sure all the doors to the church were locked so I would have complete privacy. Then he went back to the church office and waited for my call.

The lights were turned down low in the

sanctuary, the sun came through the stained glass windows and front entrance and lit up the church. This was perfect for prayer and for just being in the presence of God.

Father was gracious enough to give me the homily for the funeral mass so I could read it ahead of time. As I began to read the homily, I started to weep. Suddenly I felt Michael's presence on the bench behind me. I had a quick vision of him sitting there and listening as I read. I felt comforted by this. I could almost see him there.

Shortly after reading, I got up and walked to the front of the church. As I walked past the altar to go to the Blessed Mary statue and pray, I felt Michael again, this time behind me. I saw a vision of him dressed in white following me. I proceeded to the statue and put my knees on the kneeler in front of the Mary statue and began to pray. When I was finished, I went back to my seat in the second row and called our priest to come and get me.

As I started to call him, I noticed that he had already made his way into the sanctuary. He seemed disturbed as he approached me—flustered maybe. I couldn't figure out why. He later explained that he had been watching me on the surveillance cameras to make sure no one came in and disturbed me. As he watched, he thought he saw someone come into the church with me.

"I felt Michael as I prayed," I told him. "Do you think it was him? That it was Michael you saw?"

"I saw a man in a uniform walk past the altar and toward the pews on the left near the Mary statue," he said. "The man walked toward the pews and then seemed to walk through them and was gone."

"Michael just visited me." I felt the pain in my heart leave for a moment. Michael had been there with me. He was there for me when I needed him most, not in body, but in spirit. I believe with all my heart that Michael made sure Father saw him. He knew I needed some kind of sign—some confirmation—that he was still with me. He gave me that sign, and I will always be grateful for it.

There were other things to do before the funeral other than going to the church where we would all remember Michael's life. There was the first time in the funeral home. Jessica went with me. We walked in together and then sat down on a sofa. "I can't believe we are doing this," she said as we waited.

I agreed. It felt like a dream. So surreal.

We walked into the room where they had placed Michael, and we fell silent. At that point, I was still trying to decide whether to look into the casket. Ezra and my parents strongly suggested against it. Everyone was worried what it would do to me if I did look in.

I could tell Ezra was nervous about what decision I would make. I knew why. I had looked at his casket and realized that it was not long enough for him to fit in. I was aware that he was not completely there, and that thought crippled me. I wanted so badly to see him one last time—to see him the way he was the last time we saw him when we dropped him off at the airport so I could put my hands on his face and kiss his cheek one last time. I had been crying, and he kissed me ever so gently with our children looking on. He came back to me after hugging and kissing our children and kissed me again. "I can taste your tears," he whispered as he kissed me one last time.

That was the last thing he said to me in person. I would never hear his voice in the same room again, or feel his lips on mine. All I wanted was to see him. But I wouldn't be able to do that. As I sat on the small couch in the room where his casket lay, I heard Michael tell my heart not to open the casket. I listened to him and promised everyone I wouldn't look. When I heard my husband's voice tell me no, I obeyed.

The night before the burial, I went to the funeral home to visit him one last time before they put him in the ground. It was late at night, and I wanted to be with him again. I wanted to be with him as much as I could in any way I could. I had requested someone watch Michael through the night because I didn't want him to be alone. His army brothers agreed to take shifts as he lay in his "bed." My heart still would not allow for me to say *casket.* I knew someone would be at the funeral home, so I called our priest and asked if he could come get me to take me there, just one last time. He came right away and took me.

It was so quiet in the room.

"Do you mind if I'm alone with him for a little bit?" I asked.

Everyone agreed to let me do that, but with worry. They were all still concerned that I would look into the casket.

I placed a small stool next to his "bed" and leaned my head against it. I tried to rest my eyes, but I just couldn't. I was so tired, and every part of me ached. I got up at one point and hugged the casket really tight, trying to feel him somehow, desperate to feel some kind of connection. As I clutched at the cool smooth wood, I wasn't feeling what I wanted at first. I then hugged the other end and suddenly felt him. I wondered why. *Isn't this where his feet would be?* I later found that his casket had been turned around to keep me from looking. So when I felt that connection, my head was where his chest would have been. I squeezed so hard and didn't want to let go. I knew he was in there and didn't want to miss my last chance to be so close to him. I tried to sleep as I lay my head on his chest, but I couldn't keep my balance. I wanted to recreate the way I used to fall asleep on his chest at bedtime and listen to his heartbeat. I just wanted that feeling one more time, even if the lid to the casket was between us. I was hoping by some miracle I would hear his heartbeat, if just for a second. I didn't want to let go, ever again.

The kids and I had gone shopping for Michael not long before he died. It was almost Valentine's Day, so I got him a Valentine's card. I wanted to give it to him in person, but instead I had to put it in his casket. Before his funeral, I passed the card around so everyone could read it. I wanted them to see how much I loved him and how much he meant to me. I had never done this before, but for some reason, in the midst of all the grieving, I felt the need to share this. Since he couldn't read it, I wanted the people who loved him and mourned for him with me to read it. I couldn't watch him open the card, but I could watch them open it. I needed that to happen. I needed to see that card opened.

———— ◆◆◆ ————

Watching the dirt being poured on top of his casket was yet another heart-wrenching experience that no one could have prepared me for. The limo I was in with my children and Ezra stopped for a minute so I could watch this. As I watched clumps of dirt burst on top of the shining casket, I couldn't believe my husband was going to have to stay under the ground like that. He needed to be in our bed with the covers on him to stay warm. *Will he be cold since it's wintertime? Does he know what's happening? Does he know I hate doing this to him?*

I wanted him to come home with me and the kids. I wanted to listen to him ask our daughter, "Who is my baby girl?" And I wanted to watch her light up and shout, "It's me, it's me, it's me!" as she giggled and tapped her chest. The people who killed my husband didn't know him or the beautiful children he had waiting at home for him. That little girl who squealed in response to her daddy's questions had gone shopping for her dad just days before we heard of his death. He was going to be able to come home soon for a quick visit right at Valentine's Day, and she wanted to bake for him. We bought a little apron so that she could be a big girl for her daddy.

My daughter will never hand her father a cupcake she made herself now. I will forever miss that.

I also wanted to hear his voice echo the words, "Here she comes—Mrs. America!" as I walked through the house in my pajamas in the morning. I wanted to feel the safety I could only feel when he wrapped me in his arms and kissed me on top of the head.

Watching the earth pile on top of him made it all so final. I wouldn't let it be. I knew he wouldn't leave me and the kids.

I continued to talk to him so he would know I had not forgotten him. I told the kids he is still here in spirit. We should not hurt his feelings; we should let him know that we are still here for him as well. I told them he needed to know he is still a husband and father and very much needed. My thought was that he could help us even more from heaven.

I need you, Michael, now even more than ever. I still love you. You are still my best friend. I can't do this without you. You must know that. Please watch over us and protect us from harm. Please protect us from evil—especially since evil has already taken you, hoping to destroy the rest of our family. This evil has taken the light out of our children's eyes. I will work for the rest of my life to bring the light back.

1986 Photo booth at Carnival

April 4, 2006 Sendoff Ceremony from Camp Joseph T. Robinson

August 27, 2006 Leadership Visit preparing to depart Fort Hood for Iraq

February 1, 2007 Arkansas State Veterans Cemetery

January 26, 2007 Camp Victory, Baghdad, Iraq

January 26, 2007 Memorial Service at Camp Victory, Baghdad, Iraq

Michael and his baby girl, Meredith

Michael and Justin

Michael and Meredith

Michael in Iraq

Michael next to his Black-hawk

Michael with Justin while at flight school

Michael, Justin and Meredith on the 4th of July

Michael's Casket arriving at Camp Joseph T. Robinson

*Patriot Guard watching over the arrival of
Michael's casket on the flight line*

September 1996 Michael and Justin

4

SURVIVAL MODE

Soon after the funeral, I began to "see" Michael everywhere. At first, in literal ways. When I'd walk into a doctor's office or the vet office, I'd see his face on a magazine. It was hard enough to get out of the house and do my everyday duties. When I came face-to-face with a reminder like that, it would stop me in my tracks. It felt like my pain followed me wherever I went.

When I came home from the memorial at Arlington National Cemetery for Michael and the eleven others who died with him that day, I saw a newspaper lying on an empty bench at the airport. I glanced at it and was stunned. I snatched it up and saw myself and the children on the front cover. I had the flag in my lap looking down and my children stood next to me. We were saying a second goodbye at Arlington. This memorial was for the unidentifiable remains of all twelve of the fallen. What could not be identified was put into the same casket. A beautiful headstone had all twelve names on it in honor of all our fallen angels.

Even when the newspapers no longer had images of Michael or me on them, I kept seeing him. But instead of images, I thought I saw him—Michael—alive.

I couldn't understand what was going on. I would be somewhere and see someone in a vehicle, store, or park and for a moment, I would think it was him. Why was this happening?

I began to question if he was really dead, just the way I had when I made Ezra show me the papers again. My mind would fight itself over this confusion. Was there a mistake? Is he trying to get back to me and can't? Was there a mix-up on who was flying that day? Did something happen that no one knows about?

This was me not willing to accept or acknowledge he was really gone. It's one of those experiences that can't be explained by anything but grief and trauma; you have to go through it to understand it. At one point, I decided I should never move so Michael could find me. My heart and mind worked to create any scenario that could save me from the reality that he was gone.

It was all too much to take at once, so my mind decided to soften the blow of the trauma by making up wild scenarios of Michael surviving the crash. I knew no one would understand, so I suffered in silence. I began to do this more and more as I watched others go on with their lives, and they were expecting me to do the same. It was just easier this way for me. I couldn't explain everything in a way they would understand. That was impossible. This was a very lonely place to be in, but I felt I had no other choice. I would just keep fighting to get my life back a little at a time and hope one day things might get better.

My faith got me through these dark times. That's all I really had. And even with that, I still struggled daily.

After Michael was killed, I became very afraid of the world. I didn't trust it anymore. During the first two years of grieving, I developed some new habits that had never existed before. At the time, I felt they were something that I had to do; they were almost like a ritual I had to go through to deal with what had happened. When I would go to restaurants, I suddenly didn't want to eat off the silverware. I started asking for plastic forks and spoons. I was afraid of the germs that I might pick up and couldn't imagine eating off a utensil that so many had eaten off of. This just happened overnight, and it stayed with me for about two years. It didn't take long, however, to realize this was abnormal, but I still didn't want to say anything for fear of judgment.

I also became obsessed with making sure our safe was locked. I kept all my important papers in there, including the death certificates, incident report, and Michael's autopsy, to name a few. This safe housed all the special items that were brought back to me from Iraq, like his wallet, driver's license, an unused check that he had with him, and his dog tags. Every time I would decide to leave the house, I would check the handle on the safe over and over again. Sometimes I would be in the car, ready to pull out of the garage, and actually get out and check the safe again, not trusting my memory. I hated the feeling of being pulled mentally to do this so many times, but I also couldn't shake the feeling until I had done it. I just had to feel that the house and safe were secure when I left.

I began to do this with other things in the house as well—the lights, doors, curling irons, our air-conditioning. It drove me crazy, but over time, it began to subside. I talked to myself over and over about what I was doing and assured myself that everything would be okay. I also prayed a lot. I became extremely protective of my children and always made sure they were extra safe in whatever they did. I drove like a snail for fear of being in an accident with them. If I was grieving too hard to go on a school field trip with one of them, I would have two friends at least go on the field trip with them and keep me posted on how things were going. Several mothers who were friends of mine went above and beyond to help me and our children. They never questioned my over-protectiveness because I believe that they actually understood why I felt that way. This was a great relief for me. So many people offered help in so many ways, and I was so thankful for every single one of them. But still I knew that I needed to get a grip on my anxiety.

I realized that I carried with me the fear that something bad would happen to us again. I kept waiting for the other shoe to drop because I did not trust the world in any shape or form at that time. I never felt completely safe. I started putting an outfit next to my bed before going to sleep in case I needed to exit quickly in the middle of the night. I imagined a fire, a break-in, or someone showing up at the door with more bad news. I would wake up to the slightest noise and jumped at every thud and bang that I heard. I didn't touch alcohol for two or three years because I was afraid it would make me feel more depressed, and I was determined to be a good mom.

For some reason, I couldn't really trust anyone anymore as I processed my grief. I was afraid to drive. I found it difficult to grocery shop and couldn't write out my bills by myself because I had trouble processing what I had just written. I couldn't read a book.

Even going to church was difficult because I would cry the whole time. I would sit in the church and feel such an incredible void. Everyone else had their husbands, and I didn't. Michael wasn't there anymore to kneel and pray with me. I walked out after mass without him. I got into my car and had to drive myself home with our children, but there was no Michael. No one was waiting for me at home.

I kept placing a plate for him at the table for quite some time, only to realize he wouldn't be joining us anymore. I had set a place for him for twenty years, but suddenly we didn't need a place set at the opposite end of the table. I also noticed the way his side of the bed was always made, and his side of the closet never changed. The same clothes were there, day after day. There was no one there to wear them. Sometimes I would wash his clothes just to feel that old feeling of folding them and putting them away nice and neat in his drawers. I would catch myself sometimes calling out his name, only to realize a second later that he would never answer my call again.

The tremendous pain of grief would sometimes hit me so hard that I would just sit on the couch and be still. I felt like someone was pummeling me, physically and emotionally, as I sat there crying. I begged for God to help me. I begged for Michael to help me. I begged the Blessed Mother Mary to help me. I just wanted the pain to stop. I physically hurt all over. I couldn't stop the tears that flowed. It seemed they were endless and would never stop. It seemed the void he left was only getting bigger with time instead of smaller.

It was difficult to do anything for some time. The most mundane things felt like monumental tasks. I didn't want to get out of bed, let alone run errands or do chores around the house, but I knew I had to. These didn't always go smoothly either. The first time I went to the grocery store by myself, I remember going up and down the aisles, miserable and not wanting to be there. A stranger walked up to me and said, "Come on, smile. It can't be that bad." I said nothing. When I got home, I cried until I had no tears left.

Then one afternoon, while the kids were at school, I was cleaning the house and washing clothes as usual. I walked up the stairs and felt a huge wave of grief hit me right in the chest. I fell to my knees; I just crumbled. I leaned up against the wall and beat my fists against it. I yelled to God, "Please help me! When will this pain stop? Please, I'm begging you, make it stop. Oh God, please...please!"

Suddenly I felt a gentle touch of calm settle on my soul. I was left speechless. I just closed my eyes and rested in the brief embrace. I knew what I felt; it was Michael. I couldn't believe it was happening, but I fully surrendered to it. I didn't want that sacred moment to end. I cherished every moment of that gift from above. As the presence of his spirit dissolved, I slowly got back up.

"Thank you," I said aloud, and I continued where I had left off with my chores. I realized Michael was still there, and I was sure to talk to him—to let him know my heart ached without him.

I still, to this day, rarely drink alcohol for fear of depression hitting, but I have gotten a bit better at handling my anxiety and the pain. I still jump at loud noises and don't sleep well because I am alone in the house without him, but my anxiety has lessened with time. I worked very hard on my own to overcome all the new habits and fears I acquired after Michael was killed, and I was surprisingly successful. It took a few years, but things are getting better. With the help of friends, Michael, and my faith, I did it.

———◆◆◆———

Do you hear me when I call your name? Sometimes I feel like you watch me as I sleep. I try to imagine you sitting on the edge of my bed at night sometimes so I feel safe. I always have a night-light on in my bedroom now since you went to heaven. I wonder if you are standing behind me when I stare at pictures of you. Do you feel the love I still have for you? I wish I could just have one more conversation with you face-to-face. I have so many questions to ask you and so much to share. I want to hold your hands one more time and look into your eyes.

———————

On another occasion, I walked up the stairs to our bathroom. I desperately needed to feel close to Michael and decided that going through his things would help me connect with him—to feel him in the only way I could now.

I opened up the bathroom closet that held all his toiletries the Army had sent back to me. I unzipped the plastic bag containing his toothbrush holder, razor, and hairbrush. I smelled the bag and began to weep because I could smell the shaving cream he used. I was upset because they didn't leave his toothpaste or his toothbrush. And then I saw his brush and slowly pulled it out. "Oh, my gosh!" I gasped. There was a small piece of his hair stuck to the bristles of the brush. I cried out to Michael, "This is all I have left of you! I want more! I need more!" But I knew if that was all I had, I would be sure I didn't lose it. I carefully pulled that tiny piece of hair out and placed it in a plastic bag. I put it to my chest and just sat on the floor and wept.

"Oh God, please help me! My heart is so broken. Will this pain ever stop? It hurts so bad." I cried, clutching that one strand of hair. "I want to hear you say my name just one more time. I want to see you smile just one more time. I want to look in your eyes just one more time."

———◆◆◆———

The two crew chiefs who were on site the day of the crash, SPC Ben Pira and SGT Jonathan Hara— I know in my heart did everything they could to get his door open, but the aircraft was too demolished.

Later, when the two crew chiefs came home from the deployment in Iraq, they were gracious enough to come by my home and talk to me about that day. I made sure to tell them I knew they did everything they could, and I was thankful for that. It was important to me to tell them this because I knew that they had a long journey ahead of them in their grieving, and the last thing I wanted them to have was guilt. If I could let them know I had no ill feelings toward them, maybe it would take some small amount of burden off their shoulders.

I could tell when they walked into my house they were as devastated about that day as I was, and it broke my heart for them. I still think about them often and am so thankful for their bravery and always will be. I still, to this day, feel angels were watching over these two brave soldiers as they tried to retrieve Michael's body. They were his Army brothers and showed their love for him that day.

There was something healing, but also painful, in seeing the two soldiers who had last seen Michael. I realized as I talked to them— the two who had last seen him slumped over in the aircraft—that they also grieved Michael's death in their own way. It always felt like no one understood the way my spirit had been attacked with such grief, but they seemed very shattered themselves.

I knew every part of Michael from his head to his toes, and suddenly all I was left with was one piece of hair to cling to. That's all. I went to our bedroom closet and grabbed his robe. I put it to my face and breathed in deeply. I needed to smell him. I put it on and just balled up and tried to feel him somehow. I wanted to feel like he was holding me again. I wanted to feel safe. I had him for twenty years, and then I didn't—just like that. He left with no warning, no goodbye, nothing. That sudden theft of something so special made me leery of the world. Nothing felt safe anymore.

It was strange the way Michael would seem to

show up when I needed him most in those small ways. Shortly after he was buried, Ezra came by our house with a few small black velvet pouches. I had seen this drawstring pouch before when the army had sent all of his personal belongings back from Iraq the first weeks after his death. Those previous bags had held his wallet and dog tags in them. I wondered what else could be in this new bag. I thought I already had everything that was his. I had been notified shortly before this visit that they thought they had found Michael's wedding band and would send it soon. Perhaps the ring was in one of the bags.

I walked into the kitchen and sat down at the dining table with the officer. I was nervous, but I also had a very strong sense of knowing in my heart. I hoped the gift God had promised would be in one of those bags. I slowly opened up one of the bags, and I felt my breath leave me. I emptied the contents, and Michael's wedding band fell into the palm of my hand. I became numb for a minute. I saw hints of black on it from the fire—it looked like someone had tried to clean it up as much as they could before they delivered it to me. God's gift and promise had been fulfilled.

———◆———

It was a routine mission originating out of Balad AB, Iraq, at around 1:15 p.m. on January 20,

2007. They were tactically moving passengers in two UH-60 Black Hawks. Michael was the air mission commander (AMC) of the mission, in the second trailing aircraft. First stop was Ashraf MEK, then down to Taji. They were then en route from Taji to Baghdad (Liberty Pad), the third leg, when Easy 40 was hit with an RPG from insurgents who were in their flight path on the ground.

The RPG hit the aircraft on the left rear. Once hit and going down, Michael was heard frantically saying, "Mayday, mayday!" and "Fallen angel, fallen angel."" Michael was also heard telling the other pilot to get the aircraft under control and on the ground because, at some point, it was believed Michael's controls were not functional after his aircraft was hit.

There was a large amount of fire and smoke coming from the left side of his aircraft. Easy 40 then seemed to be trying to make a hard landing in an open field but suddenly became airborne again, nose high, briefly before impacting nose down. After impact, the two crew chiefs from Easy 71 exited from their aircraft before it could even completely touch the ground to assist any survivors. All twelve on the aircraft perished.

————•◆•————

I still find myself thinking about your last few

minutes in that aircraft before it crashed. I had always imagined that if you passed before me, I would be there to hold your hand and comfort you as you took your last breath. We were supposed to grow old together; that was the plan. I struggled for a long time with the thought of me not being there for you in your last moments of life. I often wonder what you were thinking. I have to believe the angels took you before you felt any pain. I have to believe that. You were such a good man, and I know God smiled on you often. Even believing this, I still had flashes of what happened to you in that aircraft. There are so many ways you would not want a loved one in the military to die, and I feel I got every single one of those fears given to me on a platter. I hurt so much for you and the horrific circumstances that revolved around your death. Someone killed you on purpose.

———◆———

I realized his ring was on him when he took his last breath. I wasn't able to hold his hand when he left, but I could hold something that was with him through everything that happened that day. This was my miracle. I put Michael's wedding band on a silver chain and wore it around my neck every day after that. To this day, if it's not around my neck, then it's in my pocket or my purse. I never leave the house without it. I feel connected to him when I touch it. It has, at many times, given me the confidence to face challenges that come my way on this earth.

I was not the only one who had been changed forever by Michael's death. My children also changed overnight. Meredith became very clingy and never wanted to leave my side. She feared the world now somewhat like I did. There was no rhyme or reason for the unwavering fear; it was just there. She felt misunderstood by her peers and only found one or two friends who truly tried to understand what she was going through.

Getting ready for school was always a challenge, and this did not let up for years. She would also get physically ill when she would walk into our church. Almost every time, she would have flashbacks of the funeral. She could see the casket as clearly as the day she said goodbye to her father. Our place of prayer became a place she could barely walk into. She had to go to church during school hours because she went to a Catholic school, and she would get sick there in front of her classmates, which only made things even harder on her. The other kids had no idea why she was getting so sick, and that made her feel even more isolated from the world.

I began to go to school with her and just sit outside her classroom and read. I wanted her to know I was there in case she started to feel upset and started to miss her daddy. Sometimes she would just peek outside quickly to make sure I was still there. I would hug her and tell her I wasn't going anywhere. She would take a deep breath and keep going. It became the way we lived our lives.

I did the same for Justin. He didn't come out and check as much as she did, but he took comfort in knowing I was there if he needed me. I became very protective of both of them. I wanted to protect them from anything that may hurt them. Justin, in return, was very protective of me and still is; I love him for that.

When a child would say the wrong thing to them and upset them, my heart ached for them. I would also fall into the most severe of protective modes. I wanted to yell at the top of my lungs, "Leave them alone! Their father was killed! He was ripped from them. They are hurting beyond anything that you can imagine. The world doesn't understand them! And neither do you!"

Our house was a place of grief, but it was also our safe place from the world. The three of us felt very misunderstood. We were in an ocean of grief that almost swallowed us whole. It grabbed us in huge waves. Sometimes I would see their heads go under, so I would snatch them up quickly. This went on every day. We were all in survival mode.

After a while, everyone seemed to have moved

on, but we were still trying to crawl through our pain. We had to learn to walk again without Michael. I had to learn to be Wendy without a husband, and they had to learn to negotiate life without a father.

Every day of this felt like an eternity. The anguish felt eternal. I felt like I was living my life with the heaviest weight on my back, and I knew there was no way to get it off. Worse than that, though, I knew my children felt the same weight, and they were only six and eleven. The strength they had to have is one that few can know. There have been many adults who could not do what they had to do. But my children did.

As I watched them fight to get through the most excruciating experience of their lives, I was determined to make this right. I made it my mission to give their lives back to them the best I could. The light in their eyes was gone, and it was perhaps one of the most disturbing sights I had witnessed. This is something a parent never wants to see. I knew I had to do all I could to get that light to come back. I knew it would have to look different because our lives would never be the same, but I prayed day and night that it would fully come back.

While all this was going on, we put on brave faces; all of us did at times. People looked in at us, and they thought we were moving on just as they were. They mistakenly thought because we appeared to be peaceful that we truly were—that our wounds were healing and our hearts had quit aching. But that simply was not true. We were grieving, but we didn't want to let anyone in. We were leery of the world, all of us. And we felt locked out of things in a way we never had. The world could be cold and harsh, and we felt like we needed to be on the defense. We were a small unit of three, dependent on one another because we felt we shared a unique pain no one but us could comprehend.

I figured if I behaved as though all was well, then I wouldn't have to go there. "There" was a lot of places—trying to put words to my grief, expressing all the emotions I was trying to keep at bay every moment of every day, saying aloud all the things I wish I didn't have to deal with. I also began to see that others didn't want me to go there—so much so that they would avoid me at times.

I had gone into a greeting-card shop near the house not long after Michael had died. I saw someone from church in one of the aisles. She avoided making eye contact and then darted away when she saw me. It hurt so much at the time, but I realized later that she, and many people, just didn't know what to say, so they said nothing at all.

Time passed, and one day I caught myself telling a complete stranger I had lost Michael. It just somehow seemed to fit itself in to an otherwise ordinary conversation.

To this day, that still happens, not as frequently but once in a tiny while. It's almost like I still need people to know about the great loss.

That period of time—the time I felt I was isolated in my pain and left behind by all those who had said goodbye to Michael with me—seemed like it would never end. I cried every day and lived my life in a state of pure exhaustion. I found myself begging God to make it stop. But as intense as it was, I can honestly say I wouldn't be where I am right now if I hadn't allowed myself to move through that process.

Nine years after I lost Michael, I hit a brick wall.

It was June 2015. I had been fighting so long to keep our lives together and going in a good direction that I didn't stop long enough to pay attention to the physical and mental signs trying desperately to reach me.

One day, I started feeling under the weather, and I got worse and worse until one Saturday afternoon. I was stuck in bed crying; I couldn't stop. I mean that in a literal sense. I just kept sobbing in a way I never had. I just felt exhausted. When I realized how little control I had over myself, I got scared. My heart was not beating right, and I hurt all over. There was something wrong with me, and I knew it, but I didn't know what it was. A trip to the doctor and a visit with my therapist later, I was diagnosed with PTSD and clinical depression. My doctors explained I had suffered a breakdown, and the breakdown had started about two years prior and slowly grew and manifested in my recent illness.

When the doctor told me I had not one but two conditions, I was completely devastated. I had taken such pride in being strong enough for the three of us every day since Michael had passed. I was the strong one, but I had to face the fact that strong people can also fall. The goal is to keep getting up, just like when I first lost Michael.

I decided I wasn't going to feel ashamed of my diagnosis.

Instead, I would recognize my strength, even within it, because I was still strong, maybe even more than I had believed.

I later realized I had just adapted the best I could to my husband's death and the way it had permanently changed my life and my whole being. Suddenly, in addition to my grief, I was also coping with depression and PTSD. All I knew before my diagnosis was that I had crying spells once in a while and would feel completely worn out. But the "worn out" finally caught up with me, and I had to face my diagnosis. More importantly, I had to understand it wasn't my fault or a sign of weakness. It was a result of a severe and traumatic loss that shook my whole being.

During the adjustment to my new diagnosis, and still today, I was and am thankful my children have done well with the life handed to them. And with the diagnosis, I was able to think about how I could be an even better mother because I knew what was going on with me and why. That knowledge was power for me, and it helped me take care of myself better so I had more to give my children than before. My children are my whole life, and they always will be. They are the light in my life and the joy and laughter in my soul. I love Justin and Meredith more than any words could ever express—beautiful and glorious gifts from heaven.

5

FEELING HIM WITH ME

The process I went through grieving Michael was such a long one. I still mourn his loss today, but slowly I am feeling myself come back. And I mean slowly. Losing a husband in war is a completely unique kind of loss—one that comes with so many obstacles that other losses may not. I don't say this to imply that any loss is easy, or that loss in any form does not take years and years to heal from. I just mean there are specifics to military deaths that only those who have lost a loved one in such a way seem to understand.

I have already explained many of those obstacles, but one I have yet to get to is the autopsy report. This was one of the hardest things I ever set eyes on, and I had to attempt it in stages. Once I had this report in my hands, it took me two long years to look at it. I was very fearful of what I might read and what detailed image would come with the words on this piece of paper. I was terrified of the way my precious husband's body would be described in it. I had to know, though. As much as I feared what I would find out, I had to know, for him. He was my soul mate, my one true love, and I wanted to know what those evil beings—these people who had lost all respect for human life and had lost sight of any kind of compassion or empathy or humanity—had done to him.

I started by slowly opening the envelope one day. The outside of the envelope had a note taped to the top of it with big black letters typed on it as a warning. It stated I needed to have someone with me before I opened it. I chose not to do this. This moment was mine and mine alone. Like so many other things that Michael and I had shared along the way, this was too sacred to share with anyone else, and I wasn't going to do it.

I started by pulling it out slowly, but then halfway through, something changed. It was like dipping your toe into a freezing cold pool and then suddenly deciding to plunge in because you know if you don't, you'll just run for the warmth of a cozy towel and never get into the water. My eyes darted quickly across the first line. That one sentence hurt so badly that I slid the paper quickly back into the envelope and cried my eyes out. One line did this to me. It pierced my heart and went straight into my soul.

I sat and stared at the wall as tears poured from my burning eyes. I cried to God, "Father, please help me." I meant that so sincerely. I needed God so much in that moment. I needed only God because God was the only One who could comfort me then. I fought the images the single line of text tried to put in my head. I had to believe the angels took him before the impact. I made myself watch Michael soar up to heaven before he could feel any pain. I knew in my heart that God would never allow such a wonderful man to suffer. I knew he had to be gone before he could feel anything that was described in the terrible envelope I held in my shaking hands.

As I sat staring blankly ahead and fighting my worst nightmares, I also struggled with the initial shock of losing my husband. I relived that first day in a few quick seconds—the day uniformed men showed up as I made spaghetti, the day that I woke up a wife and went to bed a widow. How could someone be here one minute and disappear completely the next? How could life change so much in such a small amount of time? And how could another human being do this? How could it be another person—with a mother, father, and maybe even children, just like me—do this to our family? How could they just disrupt so many people's lives so completely without ever even knowing who we are?

Michael lost his life in such a violent way, and the people who took it didn't even know what his face looked like. They didn't know Michael was a soft and gentle soul, nor that he had a quiet confidence about him. They had no idea he was a strong protector of his family but also a tenderhearted father. They had no idea how he loved taking Meredith and Justin for rides in the truck, even if he was just running errands. He told me once, while all four of us were on a road trip, that the most important thing to him was in this car. They also didn't realize he was a man who had once been a child, and that he still loved his parents. They knew nothing about his thoughts about life, or about God, or how badly he wanted to be a good father and husband. There was so much to Michael they didn't know.

Michael was mischievous at times and loved playing tricks on people. He was also sensitive and often felt a bit like an outsider. He respected others as long as they respected him and acted in a respectable manner. He had no tolerance for people who lived dishonorable lives, however, and wanted me to be leery of these kinds of people, too. He was always arming me with knowledge of those around me. Michael just seemed to have it right in so many areas of his life.

One day, I told him I knew he would go to heaven first because he was such a better person than I was. Sometimes I feel that God took him that day because he was so close to being perfect. His job was done here, and God needed him to fight the wars between good and evil in heaven. I imagine him fighting next to St. Michael the archangel. When you are married to a man like this, who seems to fit you like a glove, the loss is catastrophic. Reading about the details of his death and thinking that people who knew none of these things about him was just too much for me to take at one time. So that day, two years after I received the autopsy, I put it away after a single line.

I talked to Michael aloud and told him I knew he was whole in heaven. I eventually read the whole report, but I had to do it over time. Every single time I opened the letter and read another line, I wished I had been there for him. I thought about how he died without me. That thought haunted me. I felt horribly guilty about this for a long time. I closed my eyes and began to remember how he looked when he was here with me and the kids.

———————

I think, at some point, Michael may have had a feeling that he would not come home. One afternoon when we were Skyping, I told him I had this feeling that I may never see him again. It just came out of my mouth. He assured me that I would see him again. This conversation haunts me to this day.

I know he started to withdraw the last month of his life in Iraq. He spent a lot of his free time in his room and to himself. It was almost as if he was beginning to wear down. Things were turning out a little differently than he expected. I could tell by how he would look at me on the computer screen that he missed us horribly and wanted so much to come home for his R&R visit.

He Skyped me close to Christmas, and I could see he had the robe on that I had recently sent him. I could also see the small Christmas tree in the background that I had mailed him. He opened the rest of the gifts I sent him while I was watching. Something wasn't right. I could tell right away. He seemed to be forcing a smile, and his voice was dull. I knew he would tell me what was going on when he came home. He never wanted to worry me, but I knew him too well and could see something was not right. I often wonder if he had a deep-rooted gut feeling that he may not come home to me. They say sometimes people will get a feeling they may die.

The night before he died, we Skyped. Before he

let me go, he looked at me with the most loving eyes, but also with great sadness. They say the eyes are the windows to the soul and his soul spoke to me without words. It was almost a silent, *I'm sorry.* He was trying to tell me so much with his eyes, so very much. When we hung up, I had a horrible feeling in the pit of my stomach and couldn't sleep very well. Michael always said he thought our souls could touch each other when we were apart. I think our souls touched that evening. This type of love happens only once in a lifetime. Some never get to experience it.

I still think about how Michael and I would dance with no music. The kids would be running in and out of the room, and we wouldn't skip a beat. He would move so gently and lovingly; we would create our own little bubble of quiet. I remember thinking, *My husband is actually taking the time to do this with me. I am truly blessed.* It may have only lasted for a few minutes, but those few minutes would be with me forever.

One day, after we had buried Michael, I stood in front of a window in our bedroom and closed my eyes. I wrapped my arms around myself and swayed back and forth. I reached for that memory of us slow dancing and smiled just for a second. I was hoping he would join me in spirit.

For a while, I would also try to recreate my

mornings as if he were still alive. I would go downstairs every morning and turn the weather channel on like he did in the morning before he went to work. I would sit down with my coffee and imagine him sitting in his spot on the sofa having coffee with me. It is such an odd and empty feeling to make this change, so surreal, heartbreaking at times—realizing you only have to make one side of the bed now; only one side of the double bathroom sink gets used. His clothes never would leave their hangers again; his shoes would never move.

His voice was gone from our home. I would never again hear the garage door open in the evening to let me know he was home from work. I had no one to talk to now when I lay my head down on my pillow at night. There were just so many things. There were so many good memories of simple things that I missed—the smell of the grill and fresh-cut grass in the summer after he had worked in the yard, him playing water guns with Justin in the front yard, or hiding in the dark upstairs when it was bedtime, waiting to jump out at me to scare me to death. I even missed watching him talk on the phone with someone whom he had little patience for at that moment and rolling his eyes to tell me how that conversation was going.

Even though I will never experience those things anymore, I have found Michael in little things. The third year after his death, the kids and I were in the car driving to my parents on what I call a "bluebird" day—bright blue skies and no clouds. As we were driving, I saw two white doves fly right over the hood of the car. My first thought was there must be a wedding nearby. Then I realized those doves were Michael and me; they were his way of speaking to me. I also saw them as a sign that God was with us, telling us everything would be okay.

———◆———

Even as I mourn, I stand tall with the mark of tragedy on my heart and life. Your spirit guides my spirit every day. You are my protection; your fallen angel wings are wrapped around me and our children. I talk to you in my dreams, and you visit with me. You inspire me to continue living well for you and our children. I feel your presence and smell your scent on any given day. I purposely stand still as I gaze out the window and wait for you to hold me. I wrap my arms around myself and grin knowing you will join me. I still dance with no music like we used to. I put my arms out and imagine you there, and then I feel your presence. I can smile now when I think about you. Sometimes when I laugh with the kids, I swear I can hear you giggle from the distance. We may not say your name, but you are in our hearts during those bonding moments. You are us, and we are you.

I fight back with my never-ending love for you. Yes, strangers took your life here on earth, but they can't touch you now. They can't touch what we have. It's forever and protected by the heavens above. No one can hurt you anymore. We all fight for your honor. I know your friends will never forget you and will make sure others don't. Our children will grow up knowing what a very respected man and soldier you were—a man of God, a man of duty and honor, a man who protected his family, a man who loved his wife, a man who knew right from wrong, a man of noble character, a man who now rests with our Blessed Mother in the protection of her overwhelming love and grace. A man who, even though in heaven, still watches over his wife and children every day until they join him.

I know the gate is open for us in His beautiful garden, and you are waiting for us with a smile. I know you hear me now. I know you see me. I know you guide our children. I know you still love us. I know you will never leave us again. I will never give up, and I will leave my own mark, a mark that will forever remind others of your sacrifice for this country, a mark that can't be destroyed by man of any kind or in any way. Evil took you physically from this earth, but God has you forever, and that means I do, too.

I came across a picture of the aircraft that Michael was flying that deadly day. My immediate response was to gasp. I could hardly believe the image I saw was an aircraft—an aircraft my husband died in. I caught myself just staring at it for a long period of time. I struggled to comprehend what I was seeing. The aircraft was completely destroyed; there were pieces all over the place, some big, some small. I wondered where his body fit in the wreckage. Where did it go? As I studied the photo, I thought about the fact that there were twelve passengers on that aircraft. I suddenly wonder how they all could have possibly fit in that mangled metal depicted in the photo. There was hardly anything there; it was just crumbled pieces of nothing. My mind couldn't accept what my eyes viewed. Perhaps I would never accept what I saw in that picture. I learned when I finally got through the incident report that his last words before he crashed were, "Fallen Angel, fallen angel!" I hear his voice saying that. I close my eyes and wince. Why? Why did he have to die? Why wasn't I there to comfort him?

When your husband dies, no one can truly prepare you for the situations that don't go away. Even as I fought to survive and to go on for my children, there were new obstacles I faced all the time. It felt as though I would overcome one hurdle just to face another. Things I never considered before became source of pain and despair. Everyday events we once took for granted would open new wounds for me and the children.

For example, what do you do when your daughter's school has father-daughter events during school hours? I never even thought of that in the first weeks after Michael's death. Then a little note is sent home, explaining that all fathers are welcome to come to a father-daughter breakfast or a special father-daughter day event, and suddenly you realize your daughter will be continuously reminded she can't attend those things because her father is no longer here. There were also father-son events that Justin was excluded from all of a sudden, not to mention fathers as coaches or at ball games. Justin would never see his father sitting in the stands. He would not have a dad to help teach him to throw a football or tie a tie.

I learned ways to avoid the pain of all the little events that became sore spots for our family. If I couldn't find someone to help, I would just figure something else out to help ease the pain and get through a day with as little hurt as possible. Sometimes it felt unavoidable, though. From something as simple as running errands to something more complex like family vacations, we would see dads everywhere. There are always reminders.

As difficult as the reminders are, there are also reminders of the love Michael left behind. My husband planted seeds of love, compassion, true friendship, and leadership while he was still here, and now those seeds have bloomed, and the children and I are now being taken care of from the harvest of his good deeds.

6

THE LESSONS
WE LEARN FROM
LOSS

This life is yours to do with what you wish. We all have free will. I believe we are here to learn and to fulfill our own appointed mission. Each one of us is born with a gift that was placed on us in the womb. We come into this world naked and fragile and leave somewhat the same way. We begin our lives exploring the environment and family we are born into. This life shapes and molds us into the person we will be for the rest of our lives. Some of us will have heavier crosses than others, and how we carry our crosses will help shape the outcome of our lives. Some experiences will be joyful, and some will scar us. These scars are often invisible to the naked eye.

How we interact with others, process our world, love others, love ourselves, and decide what to do with each day will be influenced by many experiences we all go through. We all have a story. We all shed tears. We all feel insecure. We all want to be loved. Sometimes we don't feel good enough. We fear rejection, hurt, disappointment, failure, and not being able to truly be ourselves for fear that we won't be accepted. The one thing that I try to remember is that with all these feelings and experiences, the most important thing to strive for is truth. The truth is what will bring us closer to our Father. With this truth, we see the world in its true form. We all are so much alike; we just have different ways of walking through life.

When I lost my soul mate, truth came into my heart with a burning flame. My truth is that I am here for a purpose. This purpose did not come to me until later in life because I had to go through great suffering in order to find it; or rather, it found me.

I realize the importance of waking up every morning and being allowed to share one more day with my children. I can hear the voices of the ones I love and know they are still tangible. I know now like I never have before that God's voice is the truth and that I will only listen to that one, the voice that whispers to my heart every day now. I know that some see me as having a childlike faith, but to me, that's how He reaches me. I wouldn't change this for anything. This childlike faith allows me to feel my husband around me, even though I can't see him.

I follow my heart when the Holy Spirit talks to it even if it makes no sense at the time. It doesn't matter if we understand in that moment. If we follow blindly, He will reward us with confirmation to help us realize that, yes, we did hear His voice. The truth is God. He is the way. Yes, miracles happen. Yes, prayers are answered. Yes, the Holy Spirit can come to you at any time and consume you. Yes, life is worth living. Yes, our loved ones watch over us.

If I could say one thing to the widows reading this, it would be to never, ever give up. You are capable of so much more than you realize. Time is not always the one thing that allows us to slowly heal. It's our faith that a Higher Being will help get us there.

You are not alone.

My heart is with each and every single one of you. Your tears look like my tears. Your wailing sounds like my wailing. Your loneliness looks like mine. We both will feel misunderstood. Both of our hearts will hurt so deeply. Our weary minds and bodies will both get very tired. I'm with you as you read this. Please know this: I care. I have empathy for you. My heart hurts for you. Please hang on, even if it's for one minute at a time. You will laugh again. You will enjoy Christmas again. You will enjoy your family again, and one day when you smile, it will be real, not forced. The world around you will seem pretty again, and instead of crawling your way through life, you will walk and eventually run. I know it may seem impossible, but it does happen. It took me nine years to truly feel the joy of Christmas, but it did happen. It happened in my own time, no one else's.

I still daydream about a sunny day where sprinkles of rain come down out of a big blue sky. My children and I run out into it and lift our heads toward the sea of blue. We smile with our arms wide open. Michael slowly appears from afar and begins to walk toward us with his special, tender smile that I remember so well. We stop to watch him walk toward us. I whisper, "Michael?" As tears are coming down his face, he still wears a huge smile and opens his arms wide enough for the three of us to fit in. He kisses my forehead as he squeezes the three of us so tight. Justin and Meredith keep saying "Dad!" over and over and over again. I bury my head in his chest and sigh and think I can finally rest. My husband is home, and I have a safe place to rest my weary mind and heart. This whole nightmare was just a dream— just a long and horrible dream. Then I "wake" up and wish it would really happen.

Sometimes I wonder if God orchestrated my whole relationship with Michael, knowing how it would end, knowing that our world would be filled with grieving widows, fatherless children, families in complete despair from all the losses from the wars of today. He knew I would carry the heavy cross He put on my back and wanted me to share with others my traumatic journey and how I got a little light back into my life, something I thought would never happen because the pain in my heart was so severe. The sadness and guilt I felt for my children not having their dad were even worse. No one can truly understand this unless it has happened to them—one more reason why this journey can be so lonely at times and another reason why I wrote this book.

Sometimes I think, *I can't believe that this really happened to me. I just cannot believe this. My children really don't have a father. I really lost my soul mate.*

You can make all the plans that you want for your life and have it all taken away in a split second. One moment in your life can change the rest of it, and it may feel like no one understands you anymore because *you* don't understand you anymore. Life suddenly ceases to make sense. People will try to help you in their own way during this time. Some will tell you to stay busy. Some will try to get you to go out and do things that you have no interest in doing. They tell you it's time to get better, and they may even seem frustrated they can't have the old you back. There will be those who feel they know what is best for you even though they have no idea what you are feeling. They have not experienced anything close to what you are going through, and you can't make them understand. I had to tell myself these people meant no harm before I could continue with what was good for me and with my healing.

Some people may be less intrusive; they may come up to you when they see you out and about and tell you how much they care and that you are in their thoughts and prayers. Others, surprisingly, will dodge you, turn, and go down the other aisle because they don't know what to say or even how to handle it, like the person did to me in the card shop that one day. This can be hurtful, but I learned to shake it off. Again, I knew that they meant no harm.

As long as I felt I was moving forward a little bit each day, it didn't matter what others thought I should do. This was my journey and my journey only. God was walking right next to me the whole time. As long as I felt I was in harmony with Him. That was all that mattered. He was the way. The only way.

It was rough, but I did it.

The path less traveled has great rewards. In

those days that hurt so bad, you will be shown what you are made of. I found that I was able to carry a cross way heavier than I thought I could ever carry. It's amazing what you can do when you want to survive and want to fight for your kids' happiness and well-being—the mode I call survival mode. I came out swinging for the three of us for a long time. I was determined to show what God was capable of and allowed Him to use me as a vessel. I knew and still know that others are watching to see how I would get through this. I want people to see it is possible when one is given grace and clings to our Father.

Something else that may happen is that as you draw nearer to God, you pull away from others. I found myself pulling closer to a few but also pulling away permanently from some. This was a good thing for me. Michael's death gave me clarity I never had before. I could "see" people better. This was a gift to help me protect myself.

I saw true and pure love pour from some and witnessed the exact opposite in others. It can be disheartening to witness this and realize the true colors of those around you are either good or bad. Some can be very insensitive to you and the sadness you feel. Others know just what to do or not to do. I heard stories of some of my family members being completely misunderstood, and each story would surprise me. I came to realize some people have sympathy but no empathy. This is something I had to work through and talk out with my family and some friends in order to let it go.

If you are in the throes of what feels like eternal darkness, you are not alone. I'm with you in spirit, and this book is my way of reaching out to you. It will feel at times that no one understands what you are feeling or thinking. People don't grasp how your thought processes are affected, or how the world looks different to you. You feel like an outsider in your own family and society in general because you have feelings inside you that language cannot express—feelings that no words have been made for. You may feel you are simply existing in the beginning and don't see a way out. I'm here to tell you this will pass. You must tell yourself not to give up.

Give yourself credit for making it through the next five minutes, then the next hour, then the whole day. Some days, I walked around feeling a huge hollow gap in my chest with nothing but pain in it. My body ached. I couldn't sleep, and I was just sad. I truly understand this period of grief, and please know I pray for each and every single one of you out there who are going through this at this moment. If I could hug each one of you going through this and tell you it will be okay, I would. But since I can't, I'm hoping you will read my words and envision them wrapping around you like a blanket—a blanket of understanding, love, hope, empathy, and of a gentle voice asking you to just hold on a little longer.

The sun will shine on your face again. Just keep walking, and you will find it one day when you least expect it. After two years of solid grief and pain, it started to slowly let up for me. The "feeling better" kind of snuck up on me. When I got to this point, I couldn't remember getting there. I just realized it one day. It's like having a virus and wondering if you will ever feel better. Then one day, you do, a little. But trust me, I was willing to take the little over nothing.

When someone you adore dies, you wake up really quickly. What I mean by that is you suddenly realize what is truly important. What's incredible is that, generally, the most important things are the ones that are so simple—they are the moments we miss because they happen so organically and can seem so mundane. I grabbed on to the small interactions between my family members and close friends. I began to appreciate laughter and how it sounds like it never had before. I paid close attention to a person's movements as they walked across a room so I wouldn't forget. I looked very closely at my children's faces, down to their eyelashes. I noticed how my son's mouth crinkled a little when he smiled and how Meredith walked like her dad whenever she entered a room. I paid attention to my siblings' interactions with one another when they didn't know I was watching. I watched my Mom cook in the kitchen, wondering how I would feel when she is no longer there to make family meals. I would miss the wonderful smells that filled the room as she stood at the stove. I listened to my dad tell stories at the dinner table; suddenly his unique laughter when he'd tickle himself with his own words stood out to me. I felt great joy discovering I couldn't help but laugh at his amusement in his own words. I also felt the thoughtfulness from my dad as he said a prayer before we ate together, remembering that we were missing someone whom we would never forget. I have a very special family and am so very grateful for that. Love and understanding is always waiting for each of us whenever we walk through our parents' front door—something we all need in order to get through this classroom called life.

Dear Michael,

Every day I'm here, the sun will continue to rise and set on the days that God grants me. I think of your smile and know you are with me all the time. Life is calling, and my time is not done here. I will try to live as well and as graciously as I can without you, until you take my hand again. Your sweet and tender love was more than enough for me to feel content in this world. You were by my side, and that's all I needed. I will hold on to each day as if it's my last and continue to make every effort to make you proud of me. Love endures all things, even death. It's the one thing this world has never been able to take away from us.

Love,
Wendy

The life I have been handed can be joyful as well as still painful at times. I've gotten to the point that when I miss him terribly and feel grief in my heart, I just sit with these feelings by myself. Sometimes I share with my family because that's my safe place to turn, and they understand. But other than that, I realize others have moved on with their lives, and I'm happy for them. I still silently carry the loss with me every single day. This will never go away. I will live my life the best that I can and walk next to my children as they venture out to their future lives.

I enjoy the sunrise every morning and watch the sunset with love and thanks in my heart for the life left to me. I am grateful for the times I find laughter and appreciate the family I have been so blessed with. I hope to leave this earth with a content heart knowing I've been the best mom I can be and my children will always have fond memories of me and hold love for me in their hearts for the rest of their lives. I want them to know I will always work as hard as I can to make them feel cherished and adored, and I always have unconditional love for them both.

WHERE WE ARE NOW

Today, my son is in his third year at West Point, and Meredith is considering pursuing a military career. They are truly Michael's legacy. Not a day goes by that I don't think about him, and I know it's the same for the kids, but we have reentered the life we left that day we got the news, and we have learned how to be happy, although in a new way.

ACKNOWLEDGEMENTS

I know Michael would first want me to say thank you to everyone who helped me and our children through this tragedy. So many of you were very loving to us. Whenever any of you would come visit us, even if just for a little bit, it meant the world to us. Some came on their lunch breaks, some when it was a drill weekend and you were in town, some by phone if you lived out of state. I received cards in the mail for a solid year from many to let us know we were being thought of. I would open the front door at times to find gifts left on the front porch. Some were baskets of food and handmade trinkets. Some churches sent over handmade blankets and blessed us with many prayers. Some sent gift certificates for groceries and restaurants and even Christmas presents. Repairs were made by some of you and even yard work was handled.

I want to say to all of you that you are still our family and always will be. Michael cared for all of you, and so do the kids and I. I know in my heart that Easy 71 and the other UH-60 crews did everything they could to protect Michael, his crew, and all the passengers. I know you all fought for them to the very end. You didn't want to abandon them when the aircraft came down for the last time. And for that, I thank you. You risked your lives for Michael and everyone else on that aircraft. You all were true brothers that day. Please know I have a special place in my heart for all of you and always will.

To the soldiers from Company C, 1st Battalion 131st Aviation Regiment, commanders and close friends who knew my husband, Major Michael Taylor, and everyone aboard Easy 40. God bless our fallen angels and all their families.

To my precious children, Justin and Meredith, the two of you are my whole heart and fill my life with such joy and pride. Your strength shines brilliantly, and I am so proud to be your mom. I love you both with all that I am.

To my loving and supportive parents, Pete and Lori, who have believed in me on this whole journey and stood next to me during the darkest times of my life and never left my side. Thank you for always loving me unconditionally.

To my beautiful sisters Lisa, Tricia, and Julie and to the best brother in the world, David—all of you loved and cared for me in my time of most need, and for that, I love each and every one of you for eternity.

And to my wonderful friend and angel on earth Andrea, who had faith in me and gave me the confidence to write this book. She truly knows the meaning of giving to others selflessly.

CPSIA information can be obtained
at www.ICGtesting.com
Printed in the USA
FFOW03n0021081217
43946212-43036FF